CW00833775

A Land's End to John O'Groats ride with a difference

by

Ian Stallard

Published by Ian Stallard

Copyright © Ian Stallard

Printed by:
Mitchell & Wright, The Print Works, Banastre Road,
Southport PR8 5AL

Preface

'Perhaps it could be used to raise some money for the Centre?'

Although I have been cycling on and off for most of my life and have even completed the Trans-Pennine Trail (in 1999), as well as a few other relatively long rides, I had never dreamed of doing a cycle ride of this length until we took delivery of a Trice Classic Recumbent Tricycle in our Spinal Injuries Centre in mid-2003.

The purpose of the Trice Recumbent is to allow some of our patients with a spinal cord injury to have some worthwhile exercise and to gain other health benefits at the same time. It has a few modifications from standard, one in particular being an extra chain driving a drum, which will be fitted with a rotary shaft encoder. This will enable us to fire electrical stimulation to the paralysed muscles at precisely the correct time, allowing the patients to pedal 'normally'. As the patients usually have some difficulty in keeping their lower limbs in a precise position, we have also added a pair of special orthoses to keep the feet on the pedals and provide some support around the ankles. I had talked about this new Trice to one of the technical instructors in the physiotherapy department, who is also a keen cyclist and we decided that it might also be great for a crack at the End to End. We originally planned to do the ride together, but due to practical reasons and work commitments we each ended up doing the ride on our own. So this story is purely about my own experiences along the way.

I thought long and hard about this ride and whether or not I could manage it at my time of life, but felt that it would be a great way to raise some money to go towards another project we are hoping to start in the near future. This is a partial weight-bearing treadmill system to allow suitable spinal cord injury patients to engage in safe, upright mobility very early on in their rehabilitation. This follows directly from some of the research undertaken by Professor Anton Wernig in the University of Bonn, Germany. He and his team use the presence of a 'Central Pattern Generator' within the spinal cord to invoke simple stepping motions in patients with incomplete spinal cord lesions. The results are very encouraging and other Spinal Injury Centres are starting to use this regime of therapy.

I had done a few hundred miles in training on the Trice by November 2003, mainly in and around the country lanes near Southport and was really impressed with the way it handled. The steering response is excellent and the drum brakes can be used to good effect when coming down hills, to persuade the whole thing to stick to your chosen line. I tried on a few occasions to set off the speed camera at the foot of Parbold Hill, but to no avail – perhaps the trike's a bit too low? It's not much good if you are shy either, as almost everyone stops to stare, but I could tell very early on, that it would attract a lot of interest along the route, which might in turn, bring a bit more money for the pot. Car drivers (at least, the ones that see you!) are generally quite patient and seem to

'Can it set off speed cameras?'

'First rate engineering'

think it's about eight feet wide, but I am very conscious (and would really like to keep it that way!!) that you are perhaps even more vulnerable than on a normal bike. The other thing I noticed very early on is, that my ears are at exactly the same height from the ground as a fully-grown Alsatian's teeth! It's also about as close as you can get to a human-powered submarine when it's raining, so a pair of front mudguards are on order to remove that problem. It was fine in the rain in a straight line, but as soon as any lock was applied, you were treated to a shower from a wall of water!

So what about this particular trike then? Well, it was made in Cornwall by Inspired Cycle Engineering (ICE) and is a Trice Classic. It has 27 gears (three on the front chain-rings, and nine on the rear cassette), independent cable operated drum brakes at the front and a vee brake on the rear wheel, which can be used as a parking brake or even as a steadying force as you hurtle down-hill, almost out of control! There is an auto-adjust front boom system, whereby you can alter the leg-length without having to re-adjust the chain or gear cables. No tools are needed for this operation as it is locked up by the now customary cam-clamps. The craftsmanship is really first rate and everything has been well thought out and it strikes you as being good value for money. I fitted a Tor-Tec rear rack with a few extra custom-made brackets, identical to the one on my Gary Fisher hybrid, which I had been using for training and commuting, so that I could use my Altura Skye pannier set and top bag for the

3

proposed ride. The only real criticism I have of this set-up is that once the panniers are fitted (which they first have to be) it is then very difficult to get the straps around the rack frame and buckle up the clips on the top bag – this needs a bit of sorting to make it more user-friendly. Having bright yellow waterproof covers with the panniers certainly makes the whole thing more conspicuous, but I had also taken the precaution of adding a reflective cross-piece to the flag supplied with the trike. The problem with the original one is that, once on the move, the flag itself tends to point straight backwards, presenting only a very small visible surface to following traffic. Another advantage of the cross piece is that it adds a bit of weight to the flag and this tends to make it wave around a lot more. This movement can be initiated by slightly weaving the trike from side to side if you suspect that a following vehicle may not have yet seen you.

So the big day drew ever closer for me to set off on my epic 1,000 mile ride up the British Isles. If I had a pound for every time I was told I was going the wrong way, 'Cos it's uphill all the way' - the sponsorship pot would be overflowing by now.

'It's uphill all the way'

1

Well, this is it then!
Day Zero, May 7th 2004

Following a wonderful full English breakfast at home, my wife Christine and I set off in bright sunshine for the long trip south to Land's End, with the half-dismantled trike in the back of her Honda Civic. This was a slight deviation from the original plan, which went awry as soon as we contacted our insurance company to insure a Renault Kangoo van. It had been offered to us for both ends of the trip by our great friends David and Pat Willingham of Hull, from where they run a very professional vehicle dismantling business. It seems that insurance companies have great difficulty in helping anyone with any request that their computers cannot handle. I was quite prepared to pay, but it got very involved and messy, so they (the insurance company) were told (politely I think!) to shove it! - Hence the use of the Civic. There had also been a slight hiccup in obtaining spare tubes for the front wheels of the trike, which are only 20 inch diameter; a long story but they were promised by one company who, it turned out, had none in stock when we went to pick them up. So, at almost the eleventh hour, I had to contact the trike suppliers in Cornwall, who kindly popped a pair in the post to the hospital for me to have the following day. Er, no, not the next day nor the next! So it was off 'darn sarf' without them.

We had a great traffic-free trip through Ormskirk and out onto the M6 and made excellent progress right down onto the M5. We had a short break and driver change before stopping in Moretonhampstead where I managed to get an inner-tube of the right size, but with the wrong valve (the larger Schrader instead of Presta) plus a 6 inch round file with handle to open out the hole in the rim if need be.

We arrived in Sennen, about 2 miles from Land's End, and quite by chance found a great place for B&B which turned out to be run by a couple of Yorkies (like myself!) who had both worked at the Spinal Injuries Centre in Lodge Moor, Sheffield. This was the first of many strange coincidences and spooky happenings! Christine set about making a well earned brew (where's mine then?) whilst I put the trike back together again in the garage of the B&B and then gave it the once over, with a quick trip up the road for a few minutes as a final check. We strolled along afterwards to the 'First and Last' fish and chip shop. Don't you just hate it? - I can cope with Last, but apart from the Armada hundreds of years ago, who on earth sails into Land's End these days for it to be the First? The meal however, was fantastic so I suppose we really didn't care too much.

I felt it was best to turn in reasonably early, as I had a little cycling trip planned for the following day - and the next, and the next.

2

We're off!

'That's a funny looking bike!'

I trundled away from the B&B following a wonderful breakfast just after nine the following morning, only to have the chain jam in the front changer a few hundred yards before 'Tacky Rip-off on Sea', oops, I mean Land's End, but just a couple of see-saws back and forth soon sorted that out, with no further recurrence for the rest of the trip. I had just gone over a fairly big bump on an otherwise very smooth road as I was changing gear, so that was probably the reason for the little hiccup. Following the ceremonial stampings of sheets and a few photos, it was off on the ride of a lifetime, finally waving goodbye to Christine at about half past nine.

I made excellent progress along the A30 towards Penzance with a very slight following wind. This was the main reason for setting off from the South – the prevailing winds are generally South-Westerlies. Another is that Land's End is a great place… to leave! The gear cable to the rear changer needed a couple of adjustments before it settled down following the re-assembly process the previous evening. I chose a fairly quiet stretch away from the rather busy A30 which led me on to Leedstown, where a fellow tricyclist on an almost identical machine was speeding towards me with a cheery wave. 'That's a funny looking bike' he remarked as we both came to a halt for the inevitable chat. He had recently retired from the NHS and lived not too far away, and during our conversation asked if I knew the chaps at ICE. 'Only by phone, letter and email' was my reply, and it turned out that he had been at their Factory only a day or so previously. 'Bugger!' said I. 'If only I had known I was going to bump into you, I could have asked you to bring along a spare tube.' And so I related the story of the lack of spare tube with the correct fitting. 'I've got a couple of spares in the pannier, you're welcome to one of those' he said, insisting that I took one as 'sponsorship'. Many thanks, Bill, I owe you a pint sometime - it really lifted my spirits even higher than they already were.

I pressed on, but shortly afterwards got engaged again in conversation, this time with a local postman who was really keen to look around the trike, and confessed to me that he

'Dog biscuits?'

would have loved to have sponsored my efforts, but had nothing other than dog biscuits to offer me. As I pedalled away it suddenly dawned on me that dog biscuits were not such a strange thing for a postie to carry with him - Doh!

Minutes later I paused to get my breath part way up a quite steep climb and was immediately quizzed by a group of workmen, who had been busy with the construction of a new roof on a barn conversion. I moved on again and tried to avoid eye contact with any seemingly interested party for the next few miles, as progress was being seriously interfered with and I was due to meet Christine for a picnic lunch just past Redruth. I arrived at our rendezvous at just about the agreed time and related some of the bizarre happenings over our picnic in the warm sunshine.

'Ambush!'

After lunch I picked up the A390 towards Lostwithiel (it's not really lost, as I found it quite easily!). This is where strange happening number two occurred. The A390 is quite a pleasant, if a little busy, road and in the distance in a short line of parked cars a young blonde girl standing next to a blue sports car flagged me down to stop. 'Ambush!' flashed through my mind, but there were plenty of other folk around, so I stopped. 'It's Ian, isn't it? I'm Alan Sides' Daughter, Elanor.' Now Alan, with whom I had worked at the hospital and another one of our 'Last of the Summer Wine brigade', had said to Elanor (who now lives in Cornwall and yes, I have checked the spelling!) that she should look out for a strange chap cycling along on an even stranger three-wheel contraption. I can imagine her comment to her dad about the chances of such a strange happening in the whole of Cornwall, which would probably rank about the same as Elvis being eaten by the Loch Ness Monster on his way back from collecting the first prize in the National Lottery with Lord Lucan - but here we were!

We chatted for a while before being interrupted by the local 'Lycraman' on a racing bike, who stopped to look at the trike. No offence to the chap, he was very enthusiastic and polite, but I wanted to talk to Alan's Daughter and perhaps take a picture of this bizarre event, but I had to press on eventually, as Lostwithiel was to be my eventual meeting place with Christine and our next B&B.

Chris had decided to spend part of the afternoon at the Trewithen garden centre, buying a few plants and enjoying a very pleasant walk around the grounds, so it was outside the impressive entrance that I met her for an afternoon break. We met again in St. Blazey quite by chance, as I took on water in a little lay-by, and then it was onwards and upwards to the top of Penpillick Hill which turned out to be nowhere near as arduous as the local 'Job's Comforter' had indicated while Christine and I had been chatting.

I made good progress to Lostwithiel, where she was again waiting so that we could find accommodation. I started to feel quite chilly as

'A little haven of peace'

I waited in a pub car park until Christine had done a little trawl of the town for B&B, and on her return there appeared to be nothing much on offer. We were about to continue towards Tavistock when a young chap approached and asked if we needed help. If you think about it, it's rarely much use asking local folk where the nearest accommodation is, as they already have somewhere to stay – do you know where the best bed and breakfast can be found in your area? Anyway, as luck would have it, his sister-in-law ran a farmhouse B&B about a mile away, so we duly made our way along the track and found this little haven of peace after only ten minutes or so. There was even somewhere to store the trike in one of the farm storage buildings, which pleased me greatly as I was acutely aware of the fact that I was totally

'Refuelling in Cornwall'

responsible for its safety. The reason for this state of affairs was that the Hospital Trust had very recently decided, in their infinite wisdom, that claims for all 'low value' items would be borne by themselves; as I did not own the thing, my own insurance company could not help out with cover either. This might sound to the lay-man that I wouldn't really have a problem, but you just watch them all run for cover in the event of something untoward happening! Mileage today was 65.3.

Another very bright and warm day greeted us as I packed the trike and set off from the farmhouse in Restormel (Lostwithiel), retracing my route to the A390 and then in the direction of Tavistock. I was beginning to get into a rhythm by now and taking on water and food at about the right intervals, as well as finding timely occasions to vent some of the waste products. The weather had been fantastic so far and I even got my legs out for a short time as the early afternoon sun bathed the whole of my selected route. One thing I had noticed, was that the muscles on my inner thighs were becoming a little sore, from continually, although not consciously holding my knees in a vertical position. This disappeared after the first couple of days and I've had no problem since. There is a fantastic down-hill section approaching the Tamar Bridge which divides Cornwall from Devon, where I reached 40.6 miles per hour, and with your arse so near to the ground that's bloody quick, I can tell you!

'A fast downhill section beckoned'

'Well that's Cornwall done, now let's have a go at Devon!'

Needless to say, what comes down must go up and I was now faced with a bit of a climb into Devon and on to our next rest halt at Tavistock.

We had not really intended staying there but as I approached the town centre and parked up on the pavement for a quick drink, I spotted Christine walking towards me. She too had stopped in this delightful little town and, although it was only about 4 o'clock, we decided it would be a great place to have our last evening together before she had to head for home. A few minutes later we had found a suitable spot to lay our heads and although there was no easy place to leave the trike I was allowed to secure it, out of sight, to the front wheel of a very large 4x4 belonging to the owners. I just had to hope that he remembered it was there if he had to go out unexpectedly! Mileage today was only 30.9, giving a running total of 96.2.

We strolled into the town and found a lovely little place for an evening meal, but perhaps due to the fact that I would be on my own from now on, I had difficulty eating very much. Even the following morning I struggled to do justice to the wonderful breakfast put before me. I packed the trike and bade my farewells and set off for the long, slow climb up onto Dartmoor and stopped after an hour or so for refreshment where Christine caught up with me for our last little break together.

'A brief pause on the way to Tavistock'

'The long climb up on to Dartmoor from Tavistock'

3

On My Own

It was rather difficult to watch Chris disappear into the distance without the appearance of a bit of a lump in my throat – this really was it now, man and machine alone in the wilderness – well, you know what I mean! As I approached the magic 100 mile point I felt quite happy with myself that all seemed to be going according to this very vague plan.

I had a very pleasant trip over Dartmoor amongst the ponies, passing signs to that most famous of prisons and down through Two Bridges along the B3212 before coming once again to the cosy little village of Moretonhampstead, where we had been the previous Friday afternoon. I left the National Park behind just after Dunsford and then negotiated the outskirts of Exeter, frequently consulting the GPS and at one of these brief pauses, a chap came walking towards me wanting to look over the trike. During the conversation it turned out that he himself had thought about building one. I spotted his T-shirt with pictures of Citroen 2CVs and we had a good old natter about cars, bikes and the like. I must have been with him for about half an hour when he pointed to the sky, indicating the presence of an ominously huge black cloud heralding the imminent danger of me getting my first soaking. I sheltered under some broad leaved trees for a few minutes, donning my

15

over-trousers and over-shoes for the first time as it hammered down with great big drops of rain, but within a few more minutes the cloud-burst had passed. I headed along a number of minor roads thinking about my escape from a ducking in the knowledge that, had I carried on without that interesting chat, I would have ended up 'out in the sticks' getting very wet - strange isn't it?

It was not long before I joined the A38. The traffic was surprisingly light and the air had that wonderful fresh smell after the earlier downpour. I was joined along this next stretch by a local cyclist, who tagged along at my somewhat relaxed pace as he made his way home from work, both enjoying the distracting conversation. It was one of those strange days when you feel that you could go on forever and I triked on until around 7 o'clock when I spotted the Halfway Hotel in Willand, not far from Cullompton. Thinking that there would be accommodation on offer, I parked up next to a sign which read 'Bicycles Only' hoping that the village pedant would be away for the day and entered this very pleasant but deserted country pub. The Landlady gave me the bad news that they didn't do accommodation, but also a phone number of a farm, which did and was 'just up the road'. I quaffed a pint of their very best lager shandy and had a couple of bags of peanuts, as I was feeling quite fatigued by now and didn't really fancy one of these trips 'just up the road', having been misled on other occasions in the past; but my suspicions were unfounded when I rang the farm, as it turned out to be just as she had said and I was there within minutes. Mileage today was 64.6, so the total was now up to 160.8.

'The beast of Devon'

I managed to set off the smoke alarm on the landing by not closing the door completely as I showered, but they all saw the funny side as I emerged from the bathroom with a very small towel (that's all I need these days!) wrapped around me. I walked back, fully refreshed (and fully clothed!) to the pub and the Landlady came to my rescue again by rustling up a wonderful mushroom omelette and salad (plus a few chips), even though she had really stopped serving food sometime earlier.

I was the only customer by now and she sat chatting with me for an hour or so as I tucked into my meal and a few drinks. On my return to the track down to the farm in the rapidly fading light, I was confronted by a pair of very large bright eyes slowly edging towards me, accompanied by a rumbling sound; fear not though, it was just Rita from the B&B, mowing the grass at the edge of the farm track with a ride-on mower! Does she ever stop work?

'A very suspicious young lady'

Rita was there again the following morning, producing a real treat of a very full English breakfast and generally making sure I was ready for my next battles with my three arch-enemies, drag, friction and gravity. By now the countryside was beginning to flatten out as I edged my way along through Somerset via Wellington and Taunton, with a stop on the side of the Bristol Channel planned for that evening. This particular day was quite uneventful and I felt that I had left most of the steep climbs behind for a while, making good progress along the relatively flat landscape stretched out

17

before me. I had been criss-crossing the M5 for some time and was now heading for Clevedon for my next stop over. I found a clean but impersonal small hotel in this rather quaint little place. I approached the front door and rang the bell, but there was no answer. About to try again, I spotted a phone in the space between the two front doors, with a number to ring, which was eventually answered by a very suspicious young lady who finally decided that she did have a room available after all and if I entered a secret number on a keypad by the phone I could gain access. I still have no idea where I was phoning and wondered if anyone might turn up the following day to produce breakfast – and how was I to pay? I wasn't really too concerned though, as I did at least have a clean bed for the night. I found a little corner in the yard at the back where I could secrete the trike from harm's way, but still took the precaution of locking it to a very stout drain pipe. I was using an AXA full circle lock which I'd bought on a recent trip to Holland, where they are less than half of the price of the same thing over here. On Dutch bikes there are two braze-ons on the rear seat stays to fit these locks, which I believe we used to call Nurses' Locks. As you get off the bike you simply push a lever down which slides a hardened steel half-hoop around the wheel rim and back to the other side of the lock, which in turn releases the key for you to take with you. Mine has the addition of a plastic coated steel cable (with a closed loop at one end) that fits into a socket on the lock body, allowing you to secure it to something sturdy or even to other bikes. I had

'Just a flight of a dozen steps!'

'Channel crossing'

made a special bracket that fitted on the rear end of the Tor-Tec rack to hold the lock, and the cable comes with a handy clip, which I mounted low on the trike frame. Following a much needed shower, I enjoyed a pleasant stroll from the Hotel and out through a park to the pier. Unfortunately it was a bit misty, so visibility across the Bristol Channel was too bad for me to take any pictures. I picked up some provisions from the shop at the local garage and made my way back to the digs, for a late feast and fell fast asleep whilst reading. Today's mileage had been 60.1, making a grand total of 220.9.

The just-about-acceptable breakfast was served up by a stern-faced young Czech girl, who also fleeced me of the cash for my stay as I struck up a conversation with a retired military man and his wife from the US during our meal. The lady was originally from Austria, a country we have visited many times, so that passed a bit of time before I had to load up and head off.

Somehow or other you have to cross both the Avon and the Bristol Channel to follow the route up through Wales and it might come as a surprise that you use the Motorways! There is a good, if well hidden, cycle path alongside the M5 and also one alongside the M48 over the old Severn Bridge. The latter being found only after a false start on another track, which ended abruptly at the foot of a flight of a dozen or so steps – not too easy with a fully laden trike and no chance at all if you were in a wheelchair. So today's route took me along the docks at Avonmouth with lots of very well mannered truckers very kindly assisting my safe passage through and then it was over the second of the two aforementioned bridges to drop me into the Principality on the A466 for my trip up the Wye Valley.

Sometime around two in the lovely warm afternoon I spotted an inviting butty van alongside Chepstow Racecourse, and sampled my first bacon sandwich of the trip, to be washed down with yet another large mug of tea, served up by Vicky and Sarah of Torah Catering. Needless to say I was again quizzed about my purpose for propelling this strange looking contraption and when it was time for me to pay, they said it was 'on the house'. Thanking them for their kind gesture I said I would put £3 in the pot on their behalf. 'But it's not £3' said Vicky, and promptly thrust a Mars bar into my hand to make up the difference. Aren't folk kind?

'The old Severn Crossing'

I saddled up again and just took my time along this very picturesque valley and into the lovely town of Monmouth, where once again the GPS came in very useful in finding me an alternative to the posted road-works diversion. I had to take a little break part way up the long climb out of Monmouth by the very imposing looking Haberdashers School. Two of the girls actually came over the grass verge to the roadside to ask of my well-being as I paused to get my breath – it really cheered me up, for I felt a bit nervous cycling past the great number of girls leaving school at the end of their day's scholarly activities. I didn't wish to be accused of kerb-crawling, which I actually was doing up that hill!

… 'and back into England again!'

Some time near to five, I spotted the 'Old Rectory B&B' as I entered Welsh Newton, which seemed to beckon me in an instant.

A lovely black Labrador came shuffling towards me, as I parked up and rang the bell, and was invited into an equally lovely old house with a single en-suite room just for me. I unpacked and took my things upstairs and enjoyed a very relaxing bath before coming down again to sit outside on the trike whilst making some notes and phone calls for the day with the dog, Jumbles, sitting beside me in the late afternoon sun. I often used the trike just to sit on for a rest while having snacks and drinks en route, such is the extreme comfort of the mesh seat. A further 50.4 miles today brought the total 271.3.

I enquired of the whereabouts of the nearest pub for an evening meal, but was steered away from any such thought by the hostess, who said that her husband would be glad to rustle something up for me as she, unfortunately, had to go out. 'But he only does simple' she warned. 'Simple will be just fine for me' I replied. An hour or so later Colin came out to see if I would like beans on toast with a couple of eggs, and perhaps a pot of tea? That sounded great to me as the only alternative seemed to be a long walk or even worse still, 'Saddlebag Surprise'. I was shown into the lounge/dining room, which was very tastefully decorated and had all the hallmarks of a stately home drawing room. As I sat enjoying my meal, looking out over their beautifully kept garden and listening to the regular tick-tock of the long case clock, with the dog on horizontal guard duty at my side occasionally tapping its tail on the floor if I so much as glanced towards it, I thought about

'Simple will be fine for me'

my situation – does it ever get any better than this? I hardly think that lobster thermidore for £100 could have been any more enjoyable than this feast at the end of a fulfilling day. A little later I strolled along to the small church of St. Mary the Virgin, which to my surprise was open, and sat for a while at one of the oak pews.

Herefordshire Church

I returned to the B&B and sat once more in the lounge reading for a while, listening again to the regular one-second swing of the pendulum clock – what is it about that type of timepiece, which seems deliberately to make you want to take your time? As an engineer, I have long been fascinated by clocks, indeed a few of my friends have built them. The famous life-long struggle by John Harrison to crack the sailors' ever-present problem of accurately measuring longitude using his homemade wooden timepieces (so vividly described in Dava Sobel's wonderful little book) has always captured my imagination, but perhaps the most intriguing of all to me is the rolling ball clock of William Congreve. This has a slotted, tilting table in which a ball bearing is caused to roll, in order to give the correct duration to the escapement and was invented way back in 1808. Perhaps when I retire this might be another little project to while away the hours?

This brought me round to thinking about the many hundreds of hours I had already spent on my ordinary bicycle in training for this epic journey, when all I could do was pedal. Perhaps if I could have just rigged up a little lathe on the frame I could have made some useful artefacts as I travelled along – or maybe a small workbench could have been bolted atop the handlebars for a bit of wood whittling? The only limitations are in one's imagination – or was it the imaginary juggernaut following closely behind which stopped my mind wandering? Lateral thinking has always been my thing and, indeed, many solutions to problems in my life have been found using that very method, so who knows what these flights of fancy might bring on their return journeys?

I awoke once again to a brilliant blue sky and the sound of bird-song through the open bedroom window. I showered and made ready for another mystery trip, with nothing more than a vague route known to me. I really enjoyed the breakfast and was in no real hurry to leave. I eventually paid, collected my things and packed the trike once more. I wanted to stock up with

'Daydreaming'

'Are you somebody famous?'

24

'These moments are rare...'

some more provisions today, especially fancying bananas and oranges, and it was with this in mind that I pulled up not so long after setting off, in the quaint little village of St Weonards, being enticed by the sight of the Village Store and Post Office, which reminded me of Arkwright's place in *Open all Hours.*

I was just about to cross the road, when a chap on the other side by the Post Office called to me; 'Are you collecting money?' I don't remember actually managing a reply before he started up again; 'Are you somebody famous?' He quizzed me for some time as to my reasons for being in those parts and when he learned that I was cycling from Land's End to John O'Groats, and the reason for it, he asked where I intended to start from. I explained that I had already started! – last Saturday in fact, today being Thursday. 'What! On that thing?' he said, and promptly drew a one pound coin from his pocket offering it to me as sponsorship. I explained that I couldn't take it unless he would allow me to enter the details on my sponsor form and rummaging in the pannier, found it quickly and asked his name. 'I'm Mr Powell' came the reply, not Jack or Bill or whatever to this young, 54-year-old whippersnapper, and then I seemed to loose his attention as he gazed across the nearby fields. His eyes suddenly lit up again as he located another one pound coin in his other pocket and insisted I take that too! What a wonderful gentleman – we chatted for some time about his village, in which he had lived all his life and how things had changed. I collected my things from the shop and was once again on my way, somewhat later than anticipated, but who cared? Those moments are rare indeed in this modern world and should be savoured whenever possible.

I was by now in great need of a stop to do the usual bladder-emptying thing and found an eminently suitable spot at the entrance to a field, but no sooner had I stopped the trike when a couple of chaps on bicycles pulled up to chat. They too were doing the 'End to End', but just for the hell of it, or so it read on one of their T-shirts. We took a few photos and they eventually sped off into the distance and I managed at last to pay my call of nature.

'Legs still crossed, waiting for my chance'

'The lover's husband perhaps?'

I was quite surprised to find an abandoned moped behind my chosen hedge, complete with an open-faced crash helmet. I took some details and thought that I would report it to the Police at the next opportunity, so that at least one owner could be re-united with his possessions. I marked the spot by jamming a piece of plastic sheeting into the hedge, which I found under a nearby tree, and pressed on. Strangely, I never saw another policeman or police station for the rest of the trip home to Southport, and by then it seemed an almost pointless exercise. Christine said later that it might have been put there by the owner so that he could use it to get home, another wag thought that it had been stashed there for a quick escape in case his lover's husband returned unexpectedly – we will never know!

As I entered Leintwardine I spotted a bank on my right and pulled over to get some more money as I was getting quite low by now. There was a slightly forlorn looking Jaguar saloon parked near to the 'hole in the wall' and a chap sitting on the floor of a phone box nearby – apparently making a call. I felt uneasy about this situation and stood by the trike for some minutes waiting for him to go before I could use the cash machine. As I waited, a lady, dressed a bit like a 60's hippie, crossed the road towards me and remarked that I looked like an adventurous chap. She asked what I was doing and where I would be staying and that I would be welcome to stay with them in their commune, as long as I could manage a Vegan diet! Thankfully it was only just after 2.00p.m.

and I explained that I had to press on and get a few more miles in before giving up. Just then the chap came out from the phone box and the two of them got into the Jag – and guess what? - full leather interior! Vegans eh?

The next part of my route was a little complicated as I made my way through Shropshire and on to my next overnight in Bishops Castle, but again the GPS came to the rescue. There were very few real hills to contend with by now and the countryside was dotted with small farms and a few thatched cottages. Bishops Castle is a wonderful place, but since the demise of the rail system, not particularly well visited these days.

I spotted the 'Old Brick Guest House' and turned up the lane next to it. The paintwork looked as if it might have been done only a few

In the Shropshire countryside

'Not much of Shropshire left'

hours ago and all was spick and span. I knocked carefully at the back and Rosie and Norman came to the door and said that I was earlier than they had expected – it appeared that they were expecting a group of cyclists and assumed, incorrectly that I was their trail-blazer. There was still a room 'Up in the Gods' for me though and it too was all brand new and very carefully decorated. Norman was very keen to look around the trike and even wanted to sit on it for a photo. The running mileage total had now crept up to 324.4, with the addition of today's 53.1 – just about a third of the way!

The other chaps (five of them) arrived some time later and they were having a few days away with a bit of cycling thrown in. They were all retired railwaymen and apparently do this kind of thing each year. The guest house has a Cycle Touring club (CTC) sign outside, which I hadn't noticed until I returned from the Six Bells, where I'd had a fantastic evening meal and a drink or two.

4

Men behaving badly

We all sat together the following morning for another sumptuous breakfast and they turned out to wave me off and take photos as I left. There was not much of Shropshire left and I was soon into Cheshire, which wins the first of my prizes for being the county with the highest concentration of arrogant and ill-mannered motorists so far encountered.

Most of them seemed to be piloting the latest, very clean four-wheel drive vehicle taking Tabitha, Ptolemy and Sebastian to and from private school, before venturing 'off-road' into Tescburys supermarket car park. Invariably, there was a scrape on the nearside of the front bumper, where they j—ust didn't quite miss the gate-post of Arsehole Towers. Biased? Me? You should try it sometime, I was glad to get away from them – all of them.

I thought about carrying on all the way back home to Southport, but without any real pressure of time called it a day quite early on, very close to the Oulton Park racing circuit at the Red Lion, a charming little pub opposite the Church in Little Budworth. The total was now 387.2 miles with today's 62.8. This was a lovely sunny Friday evening and I had a most pleasant stroll around the village before returning to the pub for an excellent evening meal. There were only a few of us at breakfast

'Probably the worst decision so far'

the following morning and I gleaned that there was to be a day's racing at Oulton Park as I struck up a conversation with one of the competitors and his wife. He was racing a Piper GT, a very much admired sports car from the 60's, and he also turned out to be a very useful contact for parts for a Jaguar 'D Type' replica which I am building.

The run home to Southport was not particularly interesting, except that I was harassed by a bunch of idiots in a Citroen Xsara on a number of occasions who hurled abuse as I made my way towards Warrington for a picnic lunch with one of our patients who lives in that area. I met up with Roy a little later than planned and had a most pleasant hour or so with him relating some of the events of a rather action-packed week on the road.

I was mentally working out a route that would drop me in the direction of Ormskirk and thence to the hospital, where I would leave the trike for the remainder of the weekend before starting out again on the Monday morning. As I came to Haydock Island on the East Lancashire Road, I spotted a sign for a cycle-track to Liverpool and, on the spur of the moment, took it. This turned out to be a very bad decision, in fact probably the worst I had made so far! I wish to award that particular local council the next of my prizes – the one for having the most disgusting, disgraceful and down-right dangerous stretches of tarmac ever to be given the misnomer of 'Cycleway'. It was full of dog faeces, broken and whole bottles, bricks and general debris. Many stretches were overgrown with grass, nettles and thorn branches and there were some places where there was no ramp down to some of the entries, just a sudden drop to trap the unwary. Some of the large stanchions supporting the road signs were partially obstructing the path and at one point I had to actually cycle on the carriageway, which is a very busy trunk road, not a great deal different from the M6!

I was so relieved to reach Windle Island and the Rainford bypass (A570), which also has a cycle path, but so very much different, you would have been excused for thinking that you were in an entirely different country! I struck up a conversation with a group of racing cyclists and their entourage, who were just getting ready for the start of a time-trial and even fleeced them of a bit of cash for our cause. I pressed on through Ormskirk and rang Christine at around two, as she was coming to meet me at the hospital to take me home until Monday. I was now once again on very familiar ground and I cruised into the hospital grounds at about 3-ish and had just finished putting the trike away and collecting my things when Chris arrived. A further 45.5 miles today brought the new total to 432.7.

I had a very relaxing weekend at home with Chris, rambling on about my ride since that long climb onto Dartmoor, from whence she had left for home on the previous Monday morning. I was quite surprised how well I felt after well over 400 miles in the week on the trike; no aches or pains and really looking forward to the second leg.

'On very familiar ground'

'Some simple servicing needed'

I thought I ought to spend a couple of hours back at the hospital on the Sunday, checking the bike over and lubricating the chain and controls in readiness for the push north on the Monday (17th May). The only small repair needed was to replace the small screws which attach the toe clips to the pedals, as I had lost one of those back in Devon and had effected a simple 'quick-fix' with the ubiquitous cable tie. I had neglected to Loc-tite these particular screws, something which I had done with all other fixtures and fittings (pannier frame, mudguard brackets, etc) to prevent them shaking loose during the trip, so I had only myself to blame. I much prefer toe clips to clip-less pedals, and it meant that I could get away with just taking one pair of shoes, both for cycling and sneaking off down to the pub or restaurant in the evenings. Anyway, I replaced the original screws and nuts with stainless ones and 'Nyloc' nuts. My great friend and fund raising helper, Norman Wade accompanied me on the tricycle repair-man's trip and took a few photos of me and the trike outside the Spinal Injuries Centre while we were about it. Chris did us a wonderful meal and we managed a glass of wine or two in the evening and generally just 'chilled out'.

5

Approaching the halfway point

I was due at the hospital again on the Monday morning for yet another photo call and to exchange pleasantries with whoever might be around. One of my colleagues and cycling companions from previous fund raising and 'Last of the Summer Wine' trips, Malcolm Heathcote had decided to escort me out of town and have a bit of a ride along with me. I'm not sure how we got our wires crossed, but Malcolm was nowhere to be seen when it was time for me to leave. I pressed on from Southport and up along the very familiar route to Preston wondering if he had been unavoidably delayed. I'm not too good at remembering to switch on mobile phones and generally kept it off anyway until I could plug the charger in at the B&B's, and didn't give it a thought that Malcolm would try to contact me that way.

I decided to take the little detour through Woodplumpton to pick up the A6 at Broughton. This was a most enjoyable change from the last part through Cheshire and Merseyside to Southport on the Saturday. I paused a while at the little village store and Post Office to buy some milk and snacks for my lunch, which was taken on a quiet stretch by the A6 around Garstang. Some minutes after moving on again,

'Yet another pot of tea'

'The wood-turner's shed'

a very confused and slightly harassed looking Malcolm came cycling towards me from the opposite direction. Neither of us have any idea how we managed to miss each other, but he had been pedalling like a mad-man to catch me. All ended very well a while later when we pulled into the Flag, a lovely pub on the A6 and I joined Malc for the pudding course of his well-earned lunch and downed a rather large piece of banoffee pie with yet another pot of tea.

On my own again, with a rather full feeling, I trundled up the A6 via Lancaster in the very pleasant sunshine aiming for Carnforth, where I intended to head out towards Arkholme on the Kirkby Lonsdale road, and on to my next stop with Paul Airey and his family. Paul is a patient of ours who has a spinal cord injury from a motorcycle accident some years back. When he heard of my forthcoming trip, he offered me (on behalf of his Mum and Dad) lodgings for the night if it happened to fit my schedule. His parents owned a coach-travel company, which is now very ably run by their other son and I even got the chance to have a look around the workshops behind their bungalow. Paul's Dad is now busying himself with woodturning in his shed in the garden and making all manner of exquisite artefacts from some wonderful pieces of hardwood burr. Paul's mum had prepared a fantastic meal and we sat for a very long time filling ourselves with home-cooked fare and downing a glass or two of wine. The total was now 55.1 higher at 487.8 miles.

I had a really pleasant time with them all and turned in quite late after a rather full day. Sleep came very easily and before I knew it, it was time for breakfast before packing the trike with panniers and top bag for the long climb over Shap and on to Carlisle. I knew this was going to be a slightly harder day as I intended doing the 70 or so miles over the infamous granite lump and down through Penrith to my next stop in Carlisle.

'Very handy for escaping traffic jams'

'Approaching Shap after another steady climb'

On the way to Shap

This was to be the last of my stops with friends and I used the GPS to good effect on the latter part of this day's journey to navigate my way around the south of Carlisle and on to the western side just north of Dalston.

Today's ride had been quite uneventful, except for having the usual difficulties with signs around Penrith town centre, and the earlier passing of the magical 500 mile halfway stage, but enjoyable nonetheless.

I celebrated this event with a bacon sandwich in a lay-by just outside Kendal.

The memorial plaque at the Shap summit

On the subject of signs, I have a suggestion for the planners of these often confusing pieces of information, that all signs in one town should be planned and erected by people from another place at least 100 miles away! What possible use is a sign which reads 'No Right Turn into Alfred Street' to anyone but a local? In Penrith you only know that you have correctly selected the A6 northwards when you have actually got onto the A6 northwards and not before – thanks a bunch!

I was once again getting into the swing of it and really looking forward to the prospect of the Scottish countryside and lower traffic density. I reached Carlisle slightly later than planned, but had phoned to let them know and John was waiting for me at the end of his drive with his arm in a sling! He'd told me of this earlier and had just come out of hospital following a shoulder operation. A further 68.3 miles today sent the total to 556.1.

John and Lynne have just moved into this house from about half a mile away and are busy getting it the way they want it for their well-deserved retirement. I met John through a newspaper ad! – no, not the lonely hearts column, but the 'Old Bike Mart'. A friend of mine had wanted to buy a Norton ES2 motorcycle engine, which had been advertised in this wonderful monthly paper, which we still take. I drove him up there, a deal was done and we have been friends with John and Lynne now for close on 20 years! Lynne had prepared a wonderful meal, which was again to be washed

'A visit to a toy cupboard'

down with a glass or three of wine, and we had a great evening, just chatting and laughing as we always do. John and I did manage to sneak out to his Toy Cupboard for a while to see his fine collection of motorcycles – a 500cc BSA Gold Star, a 305cc Honda CB77 and a lovely four-pipe Honda CB500 from the seventies. I don't know what it is about old motorbikes, but they certainly seem to keep us all young.

6

Over the wall

It was rather overcast when I awoke the following morning so, after a hearty breakfast and a brief spell preparing the trike, I took the precaution of donning my waterproof trousers, which, as ever, proved unnecessary and they were swiftly removed a mile or so down the road. I had to share the roads with the local commuters as I left the beautiful city of Carlisle behind and headed along the Kingstown Road and on to Scotland Road (at last!) to its junction with the A7 and then on to Longtown. This is about the only viable way to avoid the horribly busy A74, which is now a great road for motor vehicles but not really safe for pedal power. From Longtown it was a very pleasant ride with good signage across to Gretna and on to Dumfries via Annan.

'Into Scotland at last!'

A lovely small tearoom beckoned in Annan and I was at peace with the world as I sat at my window seat and rested for a 'wee while' listening to the lilting Scottish chatter in the background. Surely there would be much more of this to come?

I was suddenly brought back from my day-dreaming by the proprietress with a line from a Western; 'So, what brings you to these parts then?' Only the word 'Stranger' was missing, but I must have looked like some odd-ball, trundling up to the front of their little haven of peace in the ever brightening sunshine. I felt compelled to enlighten these apparently interested folk with a blow-by-blow account of the whole of my trip so far, but resisted and instead gave just a few brief details. 'But it must be terribly uncomfortable on that contraption?' was the by now familiar line. I can tell you all that it is one of the most

'Mouswald church'

comfortable ways I have travelled in many a year and, but for the lack of adequate cycle-ways in the area in which I now find myself living, I would buy one tomorrow.

It was on this next stretch of road where I came upon a delightful little church at the village of Mouswald. I just had to stop to take a few pictures so that I could send one to my Aunt Maureen who has a huge collection of all things 'Mousey'.

Her Husband, my Uncle George, just seems to put up with it all and it was he who gave me my first proper bicycle, which my Dad and I stripped and re-built for me to go to high school on back in the late fifties. I lost my Dad in a road traffic accident in 1960, when I was eleven, but I have never given up being interested in all things mechanical – especially if they have wheels! As I was finding a suitable spot to take a picture, I became aware of rustling noises behind me and when I turned there was a small herd of Jersey cows watching my every move. It appeared that they too were standing and waiting for their pictures to be taken, so I obliged as they were all so inquisitive.

From Dumfries the road heads in a more northerly direction, so the strong head-wind I had experienced from Carlisle was now desperately trying to push me into the path of the passing traffic as I pressed on through Thornhill and on to Sanquhar. It was approaching 5 o'clock as I squeezed my way through the busy main street, with the now familiar assortment of seemingly abandoned

'Apple pie and custard'

'Bicycle Repair Man!'

vehicles littering the otherwise picturesque road edges. I had pedalled a further 66.4 miles today, taking the total to 622.5. I spotted a small sign on my left, enticing me down a narrow alleyway for B&B at one side of a cobbled yard. I was quickly shown to a very pleasant en-suite room and informed of the possibility of a wonderful evening meal, which sounded fantastic to me after a day in the 'saddle'. I was certainly not disappointed and Josie and Angus really did us proud. Home made soup (by her father) followed by a fantastic main course from her own hand, rounded off with apple pie and custard like your granny used to make - this time produced by her daughter!

'Can you ride tandem?'

I shared the table and a few stories with a couple from Hertfordshire who were doing the End to End in a very civilised but casual way on a Tandem. It appeared they had set off some time last year and did one stretch, then returned home. This was followed some months later by another large section, before returning home again. Now they intended doing the whole of the remainder in however long it would take. I know nothing about the intricacies of Tandem technology, but when Derek told me that the front chain had suddenly become very slack and had jumped off a time or two, it was out with the 'Bicycle Repair Man' outfit to see what could be done. Who remembers that very funny sketch from Monty Python? On investigation it appeared that the front crank has eccentric mountings to allow for chain adjustment and these are locked by two allen grub screws which had worked loose.

After a bit of fiddling we soon had the chain at the correct tension and the chain-wheels re-aligned. Apparently the pedals also have to be 'timed' so that the front set is slightly in advance of those at the rear. I can't see what that is all about, but could agree with a 90-degree phase shift in order to get four even power strokes, although that might cause problems on bends unless you stopped pedalling. The breakfast was up to the very high standard of the previous evening's fare and was taken at a rather leisurely pace whilst our hostess Josie told us of a forthcoming trip to a garden party at Holyrood House at the invitation of Her Majesty no less! This was in

'Some more motorcycles to view'

Monument to Robert Burns at Mauchline

recognition of the charity work she and her husband Angus are involved in. As a little bonus for me, I got to see his motorbikes in the shed too – a Honda 550 Four, a big Suzuki and a partly dismantled Ducati, which apparently had recently spat out its dummy.

The B&B-leaving ceremony followed the by now accepted practice and included hand shaking, email address exchanging and yet more photos! Turning left along the still fairly quiet A76, I settled into my rhythm but had difficulty deciding what best to wear; there was a slight chill to the early morning air, although I was putting plenty of effort in, so the internal temperature was rising quickly. I've never managed to get that bit just right. I passed the road to Drumlanrig Castle and remembered a visit I'd had there a few years ago, on my way back from a conference in the SECC in Glasgow. The guide at the castle had proudly explained to me that the owner, the Duke of Buccleuch, could set out from that very place and walk all the way to Edinburgh without stepping off his own land!

I really like the A76 along Nithsdale and was rewarded today with a slight following wind which increased the speed somewhat.

'Well it said it was a cycle track!'

Eventually I began to encounter the Glasgow overspill and on the outskirts of Kilmarnock was further reminded of my proximity to that (in)famous City by having the good fortune to be 6 inches too far back to collect an egg which had been thrown out of a passing vehicle. Needless to say, this was being driven by a fully paid-up member of the reversed hat brigade, ably assisted by his doom-brained egg-throwing mate. Being the caring person that I am, I would have taken great delight in breaking all of his fingers by crushing them in the door of the car, had I had the chance.

A pause to admire this little motorcycle-engined kit car

7

Island hopping

I pressed on towards Irvine and out West to Ardrossan where, on a whim, I had decided that a ferry trip was needed to add a bit of variety.

I had been perusing the map during the previous evening and figured that taking the Caledonian-Macbrayne ferry to Arran, then riding from Brodick to Lochranza at the northern end, followed by the short crossing to Clonaig would be a 'Topper' idea and would put me on some interesting roads in the general direction of Inveraray.

'Lovely sunset in Brodick'

'Lots of chips'

The girls in the ferry terminal office in Ardrossan were very helpful, even giving me a booklet with details of accommodation on the island. I had about forty minutes to wait and went outside of the terminal building to check the trike over, striking up a conversation with a retired Naval weapons man from Glasgow, who had just cycled out to check on ferry times – a round trip of a hundred miles or so! Boarding was easy with the trike but I had to follow the cars and lorries and, after removing the top bag with all my valuables, went in search of the restaurant for what proved to be a very acceptable evening meal of home made (whose home?) steak and kidney pie and chips… lots of chips.

I felt that I ought to ride for an hour or so after doing nothing much at all for the last couple of hours, but in the event found what seemed to be the ideal place to rest my head; and so it was that I drew onto the gravel drive of the Allandale House, which is less than half a mile from the terminal in Brodick. The crossing had taken about an hour and the single ticket, which included tomorrow's ferry from Lochranza to Clonaig, was only £8.50 for the trike and rider. The total mileage had risen to 674.9 with today's effort of 52.4. I soon unpacked, showered and enjoyed the stroll down the hill and along the almost deserted front.

As I had already eaten onboard ship, I settled for a pint of lager in one of the slightly forlorn looking water-front bars, and was once again treated to the suspicious looks from the locals – perhaps I had been sitting in old

Hamish's seat, even though he'd probably been dead for twenty years, at least that's how it smelled to me. I didn't stay too long in there but had a little photo session on the way back to the Allandale, and on to a much more friendly welcome. The couple who ran it were from Amstelveen in the Netherlands, so we had a little chat about their country which I admire greatly. She also fixed me up with shoe cleaning tackle so that I could smarten up my one and only pair of shoes, which by now were becoming a little shabby.

It had been raining during the night and, after a wonderful Dutch version of a Scottish breakfast, I once again set off with my over-trousers on, only to remove them five minutes down the road when the sun came out.

'Brodick Bay on the Isle of Arran'

'Arran is a wonderful Island'

The views across to mainland Scotland and up along Arran were so spectacular that I rode in a very leisurely manner for an hour or so just drinking it all in. Was I really doing this all on my own?

I had some really strange conversations with myself on this trip and regularly told the sheep and cows along the route that I no longer had a mortgage to pay. This wonderful situation came about just a month or so earlier, when the final payment was made. We were quite surprised that it just slipped by without even a begging letter from the mortgage lender, perhaps insisting that we have some more money, so that they could keep their claws in us.

There is a fair climb on the way to Lochranza, but you are admirably rewarded with a gradual but exhilarating descent to the

Arran Distillery, along which I was followed at great speed by Volvo estate, its driver appearing quite content to stay behind me. I decided to turn into the Distillery car park and lo and behold! – so did the Volvo. Although I am not a whisky drinker, I knew that I could gain some Brownie points if I could buy a bottle and have it sent home to Christine. The chap in the shop was really helpful and took care of the whole process and all that was needed from me, apart from our address, was a signature for my credit card, job done!

I arrived at the slipway in Lochranza to check on ferry times and figured that I had enough time for something to eat.

'Brownie

points'

'The road to
Lochranza on Arran'

'Hopping around on one leg'

Having passed a little village store a few minutes ago, I made my way back there to see what was on offer. I love those cosy little places in Scotland. Due to their relatively isolated position they stock all manner of things which would normally need about four shops in a town. I picked up, amongst other things, some more milk and bag of oatcakes which were to last me for a full week – gradually becoming less recognisable as whole biscuits and more like dried muesli as the packing and sorting of the top bag took its toll each day. One thing which I was really thankful for on my original list of 'things to pack', was a bag of re-sealable freezer bags. These proved to be really useful for keeping things like maps clean, fruit from leaking juices, and now preventing crumbling oatcakes from getting everywhere!

I ended up being the only passenger on the floating skip to Clonaig and just sat pressing buttons on the GPS unit. I discovered that it has a 'Man Overboard' facility, whereby you press a button which marks exactly your position, so that if and when you reach land, you can alert the emergency services of the whereabouts of your lost seaman (see! spell-check does work!) It could be of great use too to walkers who have an accident or such like. I have really had a lot of fun with this GPS and it got me out of a few awkward navigational situations during the ride. You are able to find alternative detours around road-works, without travelling the often huge distances dictated by the Ministry of Road-Buggering, and services such as filling stations, restaurants and accommodation are easily located. These frequently have accompanying phone numbers, so you can check ahead beforehand. The system I eventually settled on was a Garmin G60CS and was bought new from the States via eBay for less than half the price of the identical unit in our local high street shop. It's a 12 channel unit and is about the same size as a mobile phone. We use it for walking, cycling, motorcycling and in the car – brilliant!

The little single-track road from Clonaig on the Kintyre peninsula was splendid, so once again I just savoured the moment and took my time. There were some black clouds approaching but I could see lots of blue sky behind them, so I stopped for a while, leaving the trike on the grass bank, while I sheltered under the cover of a few large trees with my waterproof leggings in my hand. Hopping around on one leg with broken branches underfoot, I actually managed to put them on just in case and then it hammered down with rain for a good five minutes, but stopped just as quickly as it had started. I set off again and tried unsuccessfully to take a picture of the steam rising from the road ahead – all quite eerie in this sea of tranquillity.

This was Friday, so I was conscious of the need to find accommodation at the earliest opportunity as I was sure that on the start of such a pleasant weekend the Glaswegians would want to come out to use their playground. I figured that Lochgilphead might provide something suitable, but as I passed through nothing really took my fancy so I pressed on in the direction of Inverary. I felt that it would

'The Dog and Duck'

have been a bit too much to try to make it to that lovely little place that evening but surely there would be plenty of places along the route.

One very tempting place came up on my left as I rounded a bend, so I drew into the fairly steep gravel driveway next to the 'Vacancies' sign. The strange combination of a duck and a dog came from around the back of the cottage to greet me, but alas there were no other signs of life, which was a great pity as it looked such a cosy place.

I had a quick drink and another oatcake to put me on and I was on my way again. As I pedalled away, I thought back to a pub in Beverley, East Yorkshire, near to where I spent my early years,

called the Dog and Duck and had previously thought nothing of its name, but perhaps it's not such a strange combination after all?

This road surface was one of the worst I had encountered in Scotland, renowned by all of us motorcyclists for its better roads and the birthplace of Robert Macadam himself, but to this pedal pusher it was horrible. The surface was very open and huge craters and pot-holes were everywhere. I could see in the distance a crater at the leading edge of a metal grid, but in view of the car and caravan about to steam past me I had to keep my course, rather than change it to avoid the pot-hole. The two front wheels cleared it alright, but the central rear wheel whacked the edge of the sharp metalwork and the tyre went down immediately. I hurled abuse at the caravanner (Bloody week-end Gypsies!) as loudly as I could for squeezing through and not waiting until the oncoming car had passed, but he was no doubt too busy watching the econometer, adjusting the graphic equaliser and answering the phone, to hear me. Bugger!

There are a few possibilities available at these times; shout for your mum, but sadly she died in 1992, ring your wife, but she was 300 miles away, or sit and cry at the edge of the road – sissy! The only viable option was to methodically go through the procedure for providing a useable inflated tyre again.

Thankfully the rim was not damaged; the tyre had one small nick in the sidewall, so it appeared that the tube was the only real casualty. I had a spare and some levers

'Snake bite!'

'Bluebells and garlic'

somewhere in one of the many pannier pockets; in fact everything necessary to be on my way as quickly as Michael Schumacher on race day. I had stopped in a field gateway, which had plenty of room and a reasonable surface to sort it out. Unusually for me, I remembered to put on a pair of disposable gloves before I started the dirty work and then set about removing the top bag and panniers, quickly followed by the rear wheel. The tyre came off easily, as did the tube, making the 'snake-bite' easily visible. I took the precaution of removing and thoroughly inspecting the tyre for any other foreign bodies that might be about to inflict damage to the new tube. The whole process didn't take more than ten minutes or so, but I was still acutely aware of the need to find accommodation as I pushed on towards Lochgair.

The Lochgair Hotel seemed welcoming enough and they had a room for me and space around the back for the trike. This was the first place I had encountered where I could not get a signal on my mobile from Orange, so I was unable to contact Christine at home or Sue Lavery from the Spinal Injuries Centre. Barbara Smith, who now does sterling voluntary work with the patients in our centre had suggested doing a 'visual report' of my progress and Sue had been busy from the start, sticking pins in a huge map of the British Isles which was erected in the corridor at work for all to see. Perhaps that's what caused the puncture? Even with the puncture, I still managed another 51.9 miles which brought the new total to 726.8.

I repaired the damaged tube in the comfort of the hotel room, to use as a spare, but in the event that was to be the one and only deflating incident on the whole trip. I had really wanted to report that I had one and a half times the number of punctures suffered by Peter Gawthorne on his End to End ride last year (None!); but I can now say that I had one more than him, as I had three wheels to his two! Once again in holiday mood, I opted to visit their excellent restaurant and fitted myself around the outside of a lovely peppered Aberdeen Angus steak. At the risk of mixing grape and grain, I washed this down with a couple of glasses of Merlot, which joined the earlier thirst-quenching lager shandy, with no ill effects.

Saturday morning arrived with a flush of bright blue in the sky and the prospect of a swift ride to the north of Oban. This turned out to be a very enjoyable day and something suddenly took me all of the way back to my childhood in Hull. It was the smell of wild garlic coming from the many wooded areas dotted around me. I had thought as a child that bluebells smelled of garlic, because each time that we took a trip with my Aunt Doris to the bluebell woods in Brantingham, there was this overpowering smell, of course it was just that wild garlic and bluebells are often found together, but I always made the association. It amazed me how a simple smell can remain in the memory for so long, but bring back such early memories of childhood.

'Childhood memories'

'Civil engineering, pity about the visitors'

As I approached Inverary, I guessed that I might be able to replace the pullover that I had been wearing just for cycling from the beginning. Chris had washed it at the halfway point but, probably due to a combination of hot sun and my sweat, it had faded in peculiar patches and looked a bit tatty. I had bought it from the Edinburgh Woollen Mill shop in Southport not long before the start of the trip and was really pleased with all other aspects, except this fading. In Inverary, there is a 'Moffat Weavers' shop, which co-incidentally is part of the same chain, and I bought the very last pullover they had in stock of the same style. The lady even disposed of the old one for me, so that I didn't have to carry it.

As I emerged from the shop, feeling almost respectable once more, a couple from Wales were looking at the trike and following the usual conversation, insisted that I have £5 for sponsorship – there are some really kind folk out there. Out through the Arch and onto the A819, I felt at peace with the world and the traffic was almost non-existent. I have travelled this road many times before, by motorcycle and in the car, but it looked unusually beautiful today with the sky a vivid shade of blue and the gorse exceptionally golden-yellow in the early afternoon sun. I stopped for a little snack of saddlebag surprise and even took a short walk along one of the tracks by the forest.

This road eventually joins the main Oban road and then skirts Loch Awe beneath Ben Cruachan, with its huge power station buried deep within the mountain. It is certainly worth a visit and you

cannot fail to admire the efforts of civil engineers or be impressed by their frequent struggles with nature. There is a well laid out visitors centre and you can take the electric bus that goes deep within the mountain to the huge cavern which is the main hall containing the turbines and generating equipment. From the gallery platform the workers beneath appear as ants, such is the enormity of scale of this installation. The water to drive the turbines comes from a reservoir high up on Ben Cruachan, flowing down into Loch Awe, to be pumped back up during the low demand period in the night – clever eh? Loch Awe was particularly calm as I made my way towards Connel, the reflections of the surrounding hills making an almost perfect mirror image.

In need of further sustenance, I pulled into a lay-by where there was just one other car and caravan, this was soon joined by a small saloon

'On the way to Oban'

'No more weekenders'

'Emergency rations'

with a couple from the States, with whom I struck up a very interesting conversation. This peaceful situation was soon brought to an abrupt end when 3 cars pulled in, spilling out their occupants into the afternoon sunshine. All three cars had their radios blaring out the same 'music' as they proceeded to drag all of their children, plus accoutrements out along the shore of the Loch to 'enjoy the peace and quiet' of the afternoon, leaving the doors wide open and radios still blaring. There were at least three generations of them and on hearing their voices I soon realised where they were from – 'yer know worr I mean Lar?' I bade my farewells as soon as it was polite to do so, and even found myself apologising for their loutish behaviour – never mind, I would soon get the roads back from the weekenders on Monday.

As I left Connel and headed out towards Benderloch, I made the decision to look for somewhere to stay on the road to Kiel Crofts, and as this was Saturday thought it best to do it sooner rather than later. Spotting a sign down to the Hawthorn Cottage and Restaurant with accommodation, I headed down the long drive towards them. There were no signs of life at the cottage, but a note pinned to the front door gave a phone number to ring for B&B. Fortunately there was a good telephone signal here and the lady informed me that although she had no space in the cottage itself, I could use the chalet at the other end of the restaurant, joining the other guests at breakfast. This chalet was fantastic, actually it was a very large and well-appointed static caravan and I had it all to myself! I unpacked and sat outside at a lovely wrought iron table in the warm sunshine with spectacular views all around. I was really beginning to resent ever having to sit inside. I had added a further 54.6 miles to the total today, bringing the mileage to 781.4.

I later showered and changed before strolling along the lane to the main road and the Benderloch stores in order to refill my by now depleted stock of emergency rations of dried apricots, biscuits, fruit, and a pork pie – just in case! I remembered passing the lovely old Church of St. Modans on the way into the village, but I had not brought my camera out with me, so made a mental note to make a small detour tomorrow to take care of that. On my return to the chalet, I saw that the restaurant was now open and, after dropping off the 'shopping', made my way there for a well earned lager shandy or two. I tucked into a wonderful meal of haddock and chips; the fish tasted really fresh and came away in succulent slices, just as it used to do when my Uncle George brought it home from the early morning boats in Bridlington, all those years ago. These days it always seems to have been chewed up and spat out into a fish-shaped chunk – progress? Bah! Humbug! I had a bit of a sort out of the panniers, put the 'phone on charge and washed my cycling vest again and then called it a night, giving in just after ten.

8

Hello Dolly!

'One of life's little mysteries'

'Not far from Ballachulish'

I awoke very early on the Sunday morning and hoped to get to Spean Bridge at a reasonable time to meet up with Roy Moss, one of the patients from the Spinal Injuries Centre. Roy had chatted to me many times before the start of my trip, and I met him on my way back into Southport for lunch on the previous Saturday. He said then that he would love to come up to the end to take pictures at the finish. Even though I had outlined the considerable distance he would have to travel he was adamant that he wanted to be there. Christine said that I should let him do that if he wanted to, but I had left it for a few days before contacting him to make the necessary arrangements in case he had had second thoughts.

I washed and changed and wandered along from the chalet to the cottage for breakfast, where the wonderful aroma of frying eggs and bacon filled the air. On entering the breakfast room, I sat with a couple from the Netherlands before being joined minutes later by another couple from South Africa and two chaps from the States. The early start I had hoped for soon began to evaporate as we all chatted over our excellent Scottish breakfast. When one of the two Americans turned the conversation towards 'Eyeraq' and George 'Dubbaya' Bush, I thought it prudent to make my escape.

The blue carpet

It was a fantastic morning as I turned back onto the road to revisit St Modans church, so that I could take the picture I was unable to get the previous evening. I was rather surprised to be quizzed about my trip by a lady who had

'The sheep made a dash for it'

arrived to unlock the church for morning service. She said she had seen a piece about me in their local paper, but I think she must have been mistaken as I knew of no way in which anyone could have contacted the media up there; I had not even given an exact route to anyone, so perhaps that will just have to remain another one of life's little mysteries.

I was particularly looking forward to riding through Ballachulish and over the big bridge, which many years ago did away with the little ferry, which had itself saved a huge detour around Loch Leven. There is a tearoom now at the golf course on the south side of the bridge and it seemed a suitable place to sample a toasted sandwich and tea, at a table outside, sheltered from the midday sun by a huge umbrella. There was an eagle high up in one of large trees which kept me transfixed for some time - I began to understand the fascination which Orville and Wilbur Wright must have had for flying. Time to move on again, up over the Bridge, only to be compelled to stop to take yet another photograph of a carpet of bluebells in a field overlooking the Loch.

Not far from here I had my one and only incident which nearly ended the whole adventure of the End to End ride. In the distance on the road stood a group of sheep. As I approached, all but one scurried off to the left over the grass verge to get away. The one remaining decided to run away at some speed in the direction I was travelling, obviously frightened by this weird mechanical contrivance approaching. I was travelling along quite nicely at about 15 mph with a good rhythm going, but was not making much ground on this wayward beast, which was darting about all over the place. With the benefit of hindsight, I ought to have stopped to let it clear off somewhere, but in the event, as I was already pedalling quite quickly, I went for a higher gear so that I could put in some more effort and speed past it. What actually happened was that I accidentally selected a lower gear, causing my feet to spin wildly and throwing my left foot from the toe clip, allowing it to hit the road with considerable force before being dragged back and under the cross rail of the trike. This resulted in my leg lifting the machine off the road before I somehow managed to drag it out from underneath. The sheep by this time had made a dash for it over a low wall and into a field - it's probably still there now! I had a searing pain in my leg, but had the wherewithal to glance in the mirror and slow down to a stop and into a gateway on the opposite side of the road. Stupid things go through your mind in a split second at times like these - the first was that I had done close on 800 miles and was not going to let this stop me; secondly, I had my mobile phone with me and as long as I could get this broken leg plastered up, I would be able to carry on without a problem – weird, I know.

When the pain began to subside and the nauseous feeling went, I realised that I had not actually broken anything. Feeling much better, I had a drink and some more oatcakes and then

'Down the long gravel drive'

decided to rub the back of the calf with Germolene from my little first aid kit. This probably helped more by the massaging process than from the effects of what was in the cream, but I was able to bear weight on the leg after 15 or so minutes of rest. Eventually I tentatively pedalled away, using the right leg much more than the left and everything seemed good enough to carry on. Apart from a slight tenderness in the calf, which was still evident for over a month, I never really had any more trouble with it.

I arrived in Fort William later that afternoon and visited the 'hole in the wall' to replenish the dwindling stocks of Scottish funny money and then pressed on to Spean Bridge, where I would start looking for accommodation for myself and Roy, who was due to join me later that evening. I was attracted to a professionally painted sign for the Spean Lodge and when I approached it down a long gravel drive, immediately felt that this was to be the place. I explained to Glen, the owner, that not only did I need a place for me but also for a friend with a wheelchair and he was sorry to tell me that the rooms were on the first floor but I was welcome to have a look. The wide staircase would be very easily negotiable, but they only had a very large en suite family room left. I rang Roy and told him of the problem, but being a very adaptable chap, he said he could 'bum up' the stairs and didn't mind sharing whatever facilities were on offer. I was really pleased about this as there was also a lovely lounge on the first floor, so we could stay up there after our evening meal.

I showered and changed in time for Glen to bring out tea and shortbread to where I was sitting in the spectacular grounds - this is the life! Today's total mileage had now risen to 831.2 with the addition of 49.8. Roy arrived about seven and after the introductions, we were off in his Jeep to the Stronlossit Inn in the aptly named Roybridge for our evening meal. Roy's Jeep (a new Grand Cherokee) is quite high off the ground, and having spent almost two weeks with my backside only 4 inches from the road, it reminded me of sitting upstairs on the front seat of a double-decker bus when I was young – a very strange experience! They certainly fill you up with good food at the Stronlossit and as a special treat later that night, there was to be live entertainment in the form

'My first glimpse of the wonderful Spean Lodge'

'Down the stairs backwards'

of traditional Scottish music and country dancing. It was all very entertaining, but as soon as we got a whiff of the likelihood of us having to join in, we beat a hasty retreat, foolishly thinking we could just escape unnoticed, but the music stopped and we were thanked sincerely for our patronage – but at least our dignity was still intact! It was not too difficult for Roy to negotiate the stairs back at Spean Lodge, which he did as he had said he would earlier by 'bumming' up them and I just guided his legs from one step to the next to save a bit of work. It was then an easy matter to go down and rescue his wheelchair, which is a very light titanium sports type.

Once on the first floor we made our way to the lounge. I made us both a cuppa and we just sat chatting until bed time. Glen and Suzanne have lovingly restored the Lodge to its former glory in the original style and it would make a really wonderful base to use whilst touring the area. It was great to have a companion again and I felt quite at ease knowing that help would always be nearby and also that by now I had almost got this thing cracked. Roy has become a great friend over the years and he has helped us immensely with our research into the upright mobility of people with a spinal cord injury, freely giving many hundreds of hours of his own time and effort.

The following day Roy went down the stairs backwards in his chair on the rear wheels, with me providing a little bit of a steadying force – he just likes being adventurous! A fantastic breakfast awaited us and then it was time for me to pack up and be on my way. There was a tiny bit of drizzle as I was getting the trike ready, but it had gone altogether as I climbed the long hill past that wonderful Commando Memorial, which had mist swirling around the legs of the Soldiers – very ethereal. Roy passed me a short time later and we had agreed on contact at around four in the afternoon. I made good progress in spite of a little discomfort from the left leg following the sheep incident the previous day and wondered if Roy might have spotted the Thistle tea rooms, where I took my well earned lunch break and once again tucked into a cheese and ham toastie, washed down with a very large pot of tea.

I thoroughly enjoyed the trip along Loch Ness and on to Drumnadrochit, where I turned North and headed for Beauly. This takes you up a fairly steep section, which was described in a book by Phil Horsley as a 'punchy little climb', yeah, right! This valuable little resource was lent to me by Peter Gawthorne, another hospital escapee who had himself cycled the End to End the previous year. Somewhere near to the top of this section, which goes on and on for ages, with many false summits, I met another lone cyclist coming the other way and we just coasted to a halt for a well earned rest and chat. His name was Bob Ormerod, from Canada, doing a bit of a tour each year in this area, before visiting his sister in Invermoriston. We have exchanged a few emails since the trip and have quite a few common interests, especially old vehicles.

'I savoured every moment'

Monday's traffic was much lighter, free from weekenders and caravans, thankfully, were few and far between. I have a friend who used to have a sign in the back of his car, which read 'Keep Yorkshire Tidy – Burn a Caravan!' Roy phoned me around four to say that he had found a great place to stay in a bungalow between Beauly and the Muir of Ord, and asked if I thought I would make it there. As I was only about five miles away, I let him book it and met him just a few hundred yards from it about half an hour later. Today's addition of 61.1 miles made the new total 892.3.

It was a magnificent place and this time there were only a couple of steps for Roy to cope with in his chair. Our hosts Pat and George made us feel very welcome in their home and, following the usual shower and change, we were ready to go in search of food. The Lovat Arms back in Beauly seemed about right, so Roy parked on the front and we made our way into the sumptuous-looking dining area. We were quickly served by the very attentive staff who, by their accents, were from Eastern Europe, probably for the experience - or am I being naïve? Anyway the food was great and it was good to relax again even after a relatively easy day. When we got back to the B&B, the owner, Pat joined us in the lounge and we had a very pleasant hour or so talking with her about this and that.

9

It's a bit bleak up here!

The following morning after another wonderful breakfast, Roy took some pictures of me with the trike next to the Ross and Cromarty signs, something which I had been doing at each county boundary since the beginning - no, I don't know why either! I was getting into less populated areas now, and before the ride started that thought had bothered me a bit, but now it was a reality, I relished it and savoured every moment.

The vague intention today was to press on to Altnaharra, but 'Roy Scout' had been for a look-see up there and when we met in the early afternoon, advised me that there was not a great lot in between. So unless I thought I could do it all in one go, I would be better off stopping around Lairg. We agreed to meet there at around four in the afternoon and see what happened. I cruised into Lairg a little earlier than expected and started looking for suitable accommodation for the two of us. The mileage had now risen to 937.2 with today's 44.9 glorious miles. The first place I spotted looked ideal as it was bungalow, but when I asked, they had no vacancies. They were kind enough, however, to suggest a few others.

An encounter with 'Mrs. Fish'

'The inaccessible pinnacle'

The one I chose was just across the bridge and right, alongside the Loch (Shin). When I enquired was shown a choice of rooms in a typical 60's style place, run as best she could by a charming old widow. The house was quite cold and a little damp and I believe we were about the first guests of the season, even though it was late May. She must have had fish for her tea that day, as the whole place smelled very strongly of it, but we stayed there anyway, unsure of what might be in store for us at breakfast the following morning. Roy drove us down into the village proper and we had a reasonable meal at the 'Nip Inn' before our return to Mrs Fish (not her real name of course, but we couldn't resist using it from then on).

We were very pleasantly surprised at the breakfast the following morning, rating as it did amongst the best that I have ever had - just goes to show, you must never pre-judge! Our revised plan today was to rendezvous for lunch at the Altnaharra Inn and this was achieved without drama at around 12.30. The car park was particularly difficult to pedal across, with what seemed to be about 1 foot depth of loose gravel and slightly downhill. Roy would never have been able to manage that in his chair. There were two very smart looking Rolls Royces parked outside, and as we unloaded and Roy was getting into his chair, we struck up a conversation with a chap who said that it was his job to clean them and that the owner (presumably of the Hotel also) had a collection of them. These were both in black; one a Corniche convertible and the other apparently one of only two 'special builds' in the world.

Although it was warm outside there was a fire going in the lounge grate and wood-smoke hung lazily in the air, but not enough to spoil an excellent lunch in the very pleasant surroundings. We struck up a conversation with a lovely lady who had been sitting by the window, reading; she had climbed all 280-odd Monroes (hills in Scotland over 3000 feet) but had stopped recently as she had to have 2 knee replacement operations. Her friend however, was on her second circuit as we spoke. The original list was compiled by Sir Hector Munro, who then set out to climb them all. I read somewhere that he intended to climb his last one in the summer of 1914, after he had climbed his second to last one - a difficult scramble known as the 'Inaccessible Pinnacle' in the Cuillins on the Isle of Skye. Sadly, he didn't make it and died on the Western Front before he could return.

'The welcoming Altnaharra Inn'

'The occasional sound of a cuckoo'

'The peace and tranquillity of Loch Naver'

When it was time to move on we had a little discussion about possible routes, Roy picking the more isolated track up past Ben Hope, easily negotiable in his four-wheel drive Jeep, whilst I opted to turn right along Loch Naver and then follow the river Naver to the North coast at Bettyhill (or Benny Hill as it became known to us from now on!) This was a real gem of a road and for me the sheer tranquillity of it all made me take frequent stops just to savour the whole thing. At one point there was a kestrel wheeling about overhead, a cormorant fishing from a rock, the occasional sound of a cuckoo and, once again, a brilliant blue sky with bright golden gorse all around me. I saw hardly a soul along that stretch, which made it all the more memorable.

Just before I reached the north coast which, at the point where you meet it, is actually west-facing, I encountered two walkers and slowly trundling past them on an up-hill section, exchanged a few words. Mike was walking the End to End for a prostate cancer charity, a disease to which he had lost his Father some eighteen months previously and had been joined for this section to Bettyhill by a friend whose name I didn't catch. He had set out over ten weeks previously but expected to be in JOG by the Sunday of that week, it being Wednesday today. It was good to talk to them for a few minutes, but I didn't want to break their all important rhythm, so I pushed on some more.

'Elizabeth's
Tea Rooms'

Bettyhill

As I headed east with the azure blue sea to my left and the eagerly-awaited words 'John O'Groats' on each sign I passed, I spotted a board for Elizabeth's tea rooms – half a mile, and wondered if Roy might spot that too and be waiting there. It was approaching four o'clock and our agreed contact time, so instead I rang him and suggested we meet there.

My first view of the Atlantic

He was waiting in the gravel car park as I turned in and was ready for a brew and something to eat as the hosts Graham and Elizabeth welcomed us into their tea-rooms, craft shop and Tourist information centre. Graham asked where we intended staying that night, to which we replied that we would just stop when I felt tired and find somewhere then. He indicated that this might be something of a problem as there was not a great deal of accommodation available between Bettyhill and Thurso. He rang around quite a number of places and eventually found us a place at the Strathy Inn which, although it would provide another challenge for Roy and his chair access-wise, was about all that was available. They certainly went to a great deal of trouble to try to prevent the two of us from having any. We were really glad that we had taken his advice, as

'Sybil!'

Isn't this wonderful?

we didn't see anything at all along the very often hilly section to Strathy, and I doubt I would have enjoyed cycling all the way to Thurso, probably arriving at ten in the evening or even later! As it was I had added 50.9 miles, bringing the total tantalisingly close to the magic thousand at 988.1

The Strathy Inn was just what we needed; a very friendly couple running it and a gang of workmen working on a water-pipeline staying long term B&B. We had a great evening with fantastic food and company, before making our way up the narrow, winding staircase to bed – if the 'risk assessment' people had seen our antics, I would have been sacked on the spot, it's a good job Roy's chair is very light in weight. The landlady reminded the pair of us of Sybil, Basil Fawlty's wife – not in looks, but in

'Distant views over to the Orkneys as the end approaches'

mannerisms and speech. They were certainly happy up there, having escaped from Yorkshire and Staffordshire respectively. Another fantastic full Scottish breakfast awaited us in the morning and then this was it – the last bit!!

I was to meet Roy just on the outskirts of Thurso for lunch as he thought that there would be little opportunity for me to find adequate sustenance and he had certainly been busy at the Safeway store there – sandwiches, chocolate buns, a new flask, tea bags/coffee, and he had even blagged some boiling water for the flask from their café – what a star that man is! As we sat in the leather-covered comfort of the Jeep enjoying this magnificent feast, Roy was getting as excited as I was at the prospect of arriving at John O'Groats later that very same day. I wanted to have a photo at the sign for Dunnett, which by now I very nearly had! One more rendezvous at Gills, and then it was a gentle roll to the finish. The man at the photo booth who puts all of the letters on the sign board appeared to have difficulty with spelling – perhaps a strange choice of occupation?

As I waited for our turn for a photo shoot, a motorcyclist approached us and made a comment about the T shirt I had just donned, which had Southport and Ormskirk NHS Trust emblazoned across the front. 'Are you actually from the hospital in Southport?' was his opening line. 'I have a friend who visits a Spinal Injuries Centre there'. It turned out that this friend was one of the patients we see for upper limb Functional Electrical Stimulation (FES) – it's a small world! He then rummaged in his pocket and drew out some money for sponsorship.

'The bottle of Champers'

The very kind lady in the tourist goody shop signed my log sheet to say that I had finished my epic ride and then it was time to load the trike into the back of the Jeep for the trip south. This was not too difficult in itself but where could I put Roy's chair and wheels? A bit more sorting and all fitted in without a problem. Roy then pulled out a Congratulations card and a bottle of Champers - see, I told you he was a star!

'Roy Moss with Ian at the finish'

10

The long trek home!

The original end-plan was that my sister, Janet, who lives near Aberdeen in a lovely place on a Laird's estate, was coming to pick me up and take me back to her home for a few days, before Christine would come up to collect me. Roy's visit meant a much simpler plan had now evolved. He would take me back to Janet's, have a few days there and then take me back to Southport. At this point I must explain a bit further; my niece Rebekah, who now lives in Cleveland, Ohio, USA married Steve, who himself has a high spinal cord injury and is therefore a wheelchair user. When they visit my sister and brother-in-law Jim, there is a special wheelchair friendly bedroom, which Janet and Jim have fully equipped with all of the necessary adaptations, so Roy could make himself at home there.

We had a great time together for a few days. Janet loves looking after folk and regularly does the 'feeding of the five thousand' bit. I even got to do my car-repairing act, by extracting a broken bulb from the clock unit in Janet's car as a form of relaxation. Roy had a great time exploring the grounds of the Laird's stately home - known locally as 'The Big House' and said that he could easily live around these parts in the peace and tranquillity of it all. Eventually it was time to head home again and we chose the rather more scenic route through Braemar and Perth to get to the M74 and down towards Carlisle.

So a little about the trip, well I had covered 1035 miles and had cycled 18 days. The trike was a fantastic way to see our beautiful countryside and certainly helped raise a few more pounds along the route, as well as relieving me of a few. I actually lost over half a stone on the trip itself, plus a bit more than that during the training and felt all the better for it.

Would I do it again? is the often-asked question and my answer is a resounding 'NO!' I enjoyed it so much and had near perfect weather, I really don't think it could ever be the same another time. There are, however, some really great long distance rides to tackle in other places.

My efforts during the ride took me to the following overnight stops:

Day   0   Sennen with Christine

Day   1   Lostwithiel with Christine

Day   2   Tavistock with Christine

Day   3   Cullompton (Willand) On my own

Day   4   Clevedon On my own

Day   5   Welsh Newton, Herefordshire On my own

Day   6   Bishops Castle, Shrewsbury On my own

Day   7   Oulton Park, Cheshire On my own

Day   8   Southport at Home

Day   9   Southport at Home

Day 10   Carnforth with Paul Airey and his family

Day 11   Carlisle with John and Lynne Bainbridge

Day 12   Sanquhar On my own

Day 13   Brodick, Isle of Arran On my own

Day 14   Lochgair On my own

Day 15   Spean Bridge with Roy Moss

Day 16   Windhill, Beauly with Roy Moss

Day 17   Lairg with Roy Moss

Day 18   Strathy with Roy Moss

Day 19   John O'Groats Finished at 3.30pm

The GPS told me that I had averaged 10.4 mph when cycling and that is just a tad short of 100 hours pedalling, but unfortunately it also gave me the bad news that I spent almost 67 hours talking, eating, drinking, peeing and all other activities when not a pedal was turned. I switched off the GPS at each day's end, so at least it didn't catch me sleeping!

It's probably obvious, but on a trip like this, you have a lot of thinking time; during one relatively uneventful spell in the Scottish Highlands, I got round to wondering how many times I had actually turned these pedals. I selected a relatively flat section together with a 'sweet' gear for a comfortable 15 or so mph and counted the total complete crank turns for a mile. I repeated this on a few occasions during that day at different speeds and came up with a surprisingly consistent answer. Bearing in mind that I was sometimes pedalling very slowly uphill and other times like a man possessed, this would provide some sort of average and not be very far wrong. It transpired that over each and every mile travelled, I had turned the pedals 500 times, so therefore over the whole End to End trip, I had turned them half a million times. I was quite surprised at that figure and it makes you realise just how big a number a million is. Modern computers can easily make many millions of calculations each second!

Another relatively useless but nonetheless interesting piece of trivia to some is that the GPS also records the total height ascended, in other words, as you climb hills it records cumulative increments of height gained, but does not subtract the downhill bits. It was therefore of great wonder to me that I had climbed over 66,000 feet (3 Mt. Everests!) on the trip.

Obviously, in travelling the whole length of this wonderful island of ours, there is a huge choice of routes available; I opted for a basic route using relatively main roads in view of the fact that the trike is quite large and not really suited to anything off-road. This was obtained from the CTC and was used as a framework on which to hang my own little deviations and detours as outlined previously. A southern start was preferred, hopefully to take advantage of the prevailing wind. With hindsight, I am really pleased with that original decision, as I would have hated to leave the tranquillity of northern Scotland behind in order to head for increasingly busy places.

Another early decision was to seek accommodation as I progressed, rather than pre-booking anything, which was fine at that time of year, but could perhaps have posed a problem at the height of the season.

Carrying a mobile phone and the GPS was comforting, and both items provided very worthwhile insurance psychologically. I also took a digital camera with a spare card to store a few memories of the trip. Having two large panniers and a top bag meant that I could take a fair amount of spare clothing and waterproofs and, having toured by motorcycle for many years, I have become accustomed to estimating the correct amount of gear to take along. I have no objections to buying an odd item or two or even to discarding unnecessary stuff.

As the trike is somewhat more complicated than an ordinary bike, I had to be a bit more conscious of what tools to carry – obviously spare tubes for each end were needed and a puncture repair kit (2 in fact) were carried. I felt it necessary to carry chain lube, tyre levers and a multitool which Malcolm picked up for me with allen keys, a chain splitter and even a gadget for removing boy scouts from horses hooves!

Recent Progress

I feel that I must add a brief note by way of a thank you to all of the very kind and generous people who donated money to this worthwhile cause. The money (over £5000) has been added to existing funds earmarked for the Gait Re-education Project and I can now report that the Partial Weight Bearing Treadmill has actually arrived, and has been installed ready for use by our patients.

Acknowledgements:

I would like to offer my sincere thanks to the following people:

Harry Newman, Dennis Woodward and Keith Mitchell, all of Mitchell and Wright, the Southport printers, for all of their much needed help and guidance during my many visits to them during the production of this book.

My Cousin Neil Holmes, without whom, the pictures would never have been suitable for inclusion.

My Wife Christine for her untiring help in the preparation for the ride and for ferrying the trike and me all the way to Land's End and also for putting up with me as I produced this book.